Lead Like Jesus

Beginning the Journey

Ken Blanchard
Phil Hodges
Lee Ross
Avery Willis

with
Karen McGuire & Jesse Palmer

Nashville, Tennessee

Copyright © 2003 by The Center for Faithwalk Leadership

Published by the J. Countryman® division of the Thomas Nelson Book Group, Nashville, Tennessee 37214

All rights reserved. No portion of this publication may be reproduced, stored in a retrieval mechanism, or transmitted in any form by any means—electronic, mechanical, photocopying, recording, or any other—except for brief quotations in printed reviews, without the prior written permission of the publisher.

J. Countryman® is a registered trademark of Thomas Nelson, Inc.

Unless otherwise indicated, all Scripture quotations in this book are from The New International Version of the Bible (NIV) © 1984 by the International Bible Society. Used by permission of Zondervan Bible Publishers.

Designed by Lookout Design Group, Inc., Minneapolis, Minnesota

ISBN 1-4041-0120-9

Printed and bound in the United States of America

www.thomasnelson.com

www.jcountryman.com

www.leadlikejesus.com

Contents

Introductory Session
{page 21}

The Big Picture
{page 26}

The Heart
{page 30}

Exalting God Only
{page 34}

Changing Your
Leadership Behavior
{page 43}

The Habits
{page 48}

Living as a
Lead Like Jesus Leader
{page 53}

My Next Steps for
Leading Like Jesus
{page 57}

Additional Resources
{page 62}

About the Authors

KEN BLANCHARD is the Chief Spiritual Officer of The Ken Blanchard Companies, a full-service management consulting and training company that he and his wife, Margie, founded in 1979. Ken co-authored *The One Minute Manager®* with Spencer Johnson, and the book has sold more than ten million copies and been translated into more than twenty-five languages. Some of his recent books are: *Raving Fans* and *Gung Ho* (both with Sheldon Bowles), *Leadership by the Book* (with Phil Hodges and Bill Hybels), *Whale Done!* (with Thad Lacinak, Chuck Thompkins, and Jim Ballard), *The Generosity Factor* (with S. Truett Cathy), and *The One Minute Apology* (with Margaret McBride). Ken is one of today's most sought-after authors, speakers, and business consultants, and he is co-founder of the Center for Faithwalk Leadership, a non-profit ministry committed to challenging and equipping people to Lead Like Jesus. Ken has degrees from Cornell University, where he also serves as a trustee emeritus and visiting lecturer.

PHIL HODGES currently serves as Vice Chairman of the Center for Faithwalk Leadership which he co-founded with longtime friend Ken Blanchard in 1999. The Center for Faithwalk Leadership is a nonprofit organization dedicated to challenging and equipping people to Lead Like Jesus. In 1997 Phil concluded a thirty-five year career in human resources and industrial relations with Xerox Corporation and U.S. Steel to serve as a Consulting Partner with The Ken Blanchard Companies prior to founding the Center. During six years as Chairman of the Elder Council in his local congregation, Phil developed a passion for bringing effective leadership principles into the life of the modern church. He is a graduate of Cornell University and co-author of two books; *Leadership by the Book* with Ken Blanchard and Bill Hybels and *The Servant Leader* with Ken Blanchard. Phil and his wife, Jane Kinnaird Hodges, live in Southern California.

LEE ROSS is the executive director for The Center for Faithwalk Leadership and is responsible for training and developing materials for use in faith-based organizations. Before coming to the center, he was a specialist for the Leadership

Development Ministries office of the Georgia Baptist Convention, where he created an ongoing process of leadership development training for the local church and other faith-based organizations. He also is a resource trainer for The Ken Blanchard Companies. Lee has over twenty-six years of experience in the area of training and developing leaders in both faith-based and non-faith-based organizations. He has served local churches in staff positions as well as serving as senior pastor. Lee has a passion to see Christian leaders across the country use Jesus as their role model for leadership. Lee holds a bachelor of science degree in psychology from Mercer University and a master of theology degree from Southwestern Baptist Theological Seminary.

AVERY WILLIS currently serves as the Senior Vice President of Overseas Operations for the International Mission Board of the Southern Baptist Convention where he oversees the work of 5,600 missionaries in 183 countries. His experience includes serving as a pastor, seminary president, author and developer of innovative educational methodologies. He and his wife, Shirley, served with their five children as missionaries to Indonesia for fourteen years. Avery is perhaps best known as the author of *MasterLife Discipleship Training*, which has been translated into more than 50 languages and *MasterBuilder: Multiplying Leaders*. He has authored or co-authored 16 books in English and Indonesian including *On Mission with God* with Henry Blackaby. Avery has a passion to equip Christians to Lead Like Jesus and to reach the peoples of the world without Christ. He has led the International Mission Board to embrace Lead like Jesus and helped develop this study guide so it can be applied worldwide. Avery holds a Bachelor of Arts degree from Oklahoma Baptist University and a Master of Divinity and Doctor of Theology degrees from Southwestern Baptist Theological Seminary.

KAREN MCGUIRE pulls a wealth of insight from her work experiences at the Pentagon, in higher education and church staff. She holds degrees from Palm Beach Atlantic University and Florida Atlantic University.

JESSE PALMER helps churches and Christian organizations develop innovative ways of communicating. He holds degrees from Samford University and Southern Baptist Seminary.

A Note from the Authors

We want to welcome you to the *Lead like Jesus* Group Leader's Guide. We are delighted that you have chosen to facilitate a *Lead Like Jesus* group study. The purpose of this Leader's Guide is to help you capture the key messages from each lesson and to facilitate each week's discussion so that all learners (including yourself) can receive the greatest benefit from the experience.

It is our hope and prayer that you will be blessed in a special way as you lead others to a new understanding of Jesus as the perfect leadership role model for all time.

As you read and pray through each lesson, we know you will be challenged and motivated to follow the leadership example of Jesus. At the Center For Faithwalk Leadership we define "leadership" as any time you are trying to influence the thoughts and actions of another individual to accomplish specific tasks or goals. We define a "leader" as anyone who has influence over another person—so whether you are a parent, a brother or sister, a co-worker, a manager, or a pastor, you demonstrate leadership with and to those around you.

This Leader's Guide has been designed to give you the tools and information you need to lead your group effectively. However, it is just as important that as the leader of your group, you commit to God that you will model the concepts of leading like Jesus in all areas of your life.

Are you ready? Let's begin.

Prayerfully,
Ken Blanchard, Phil Hodges, Lee Ross, Avery Willis, Karen McGuire, Jesse Palmer

Preparing for a Lead Like Jesus Group Study

As the leader of a small group, you will need to prepare for the study, enlist group members, guide the group, and follow up at the end of the study. The following suggestions should help you accomplish these tasks.

Your Role as a Group Discussion Leader

You may be experiencing some qualms about serving as a *Lead Like Jesus* group leader based on what you think is required. Let us try and put some of your concerns to rest. Your role in this small group is not that of a teacher. You are a leader of learning activities. You are a facilitator of the group learning process. If you sense God has led you to accept this position, you can trust Him to equip you to accomplish the task.

Group members will be spending two to three hours a week in personal study of the *Lead Like Jesus* materials before each small group gathering. During that time the Holy Spirit will be their primary teacher. The content and learning activities they experience during the week will help them learn the basic truths and principles during the week. Your job is to help them review what they have learned, share what aspects of leading like Jesus have come clear to them during their study time, and discuss how their discoveries apply to their own leadership activities.

Don't unnecessarily burden yourself by trying to answer every difficult question that may come up as you guide people through the *Lead Like Jesus* learning experience. You are a learner, too, and you should be open to saying "I don't know," then engaging the best thoughts and prayers of the group to answer the hard questions. One way to bring additional meaning and reality to the group study process is through the power of personal stories. When key lessons are taught in the video segments that you will watch together in the group sessions, try to think of situations from your own life when these principles applied. Encourage others to do so as well. It will help bring high-level concepts down to earth.

Size of Groups for Effective Learning

Jesus preached to large crowds, but He did most of His discipleship training with a group of twelve. He was even more intimate with three of His disciples who would be the key leaders in the early Church. To provide a learning environment where the Holy Spirit can do His best work in the lives of the group members, each person needs to be in a small group. In intimate community they more easily can ask questions, share personal experiences and vulnerabilities, and support one another's growth. For the *Lead Like Jesus* experience, the ideal size study group ranges from eight to ten people. It will be better to create more groups than go above this number because of the impact that size will have on the amount of sharing and interaction that will occur. Smaller sub-groupings also will be suggested for various learning experiences where appropriate.

Leader's Weekly Preparation Assignments

1. Review the subject matter for the week and complete the learning activities.

2. Find a quiet time and place to pray for the group members by name. Ask the Lord to give you the wisdom you need to prepare for and lead the next session.

3. Read the instructions for leading the next session.

4. Copy any handouts that will be needed for the session.

5. Choose any music or other appropriate media for the pre-session time.

6. Check with the host or hostess to be sure he or she is prepared for the group this week.

7. Arrange for refreshments.

8. Secure enough name tags for those you expect to attend.

9. Have extra pens, pencils, and blank paper available.

10. Secure and test video equipment, and cue video to the appropriate segment(s).

11. Plan to stay within the times given for each activity. Ninety minutes is the time allotted for each session. You may want to print out an agenda each week with the subjects and times listed. This will guide the group and allow the members to stay on schedule.

NOTE: Allowing members to share freely is far more important than sticking to a schedule. Group members sometimes arrive eager to tell about something that happened in their lives during the week related to that week's content.

12. Be sensitive to the needs of the group and be flexible. Allow God to work in the life of your group. Provide opportunities for everyone to share during the session.

Leader's Personal Preparation Checklist

As you prepare to facilitate the *Lead Like Jesus* study, here are some personal preparation steps:

1. Pray . . . for yourself and for your group members.

2. Review leader qualifications:
   - Be a growing Christian.
   - Be a person of personal prayer and Bible study.
   - Be willing to give time and energy to encourage members of the group.
   - Have a teachable spirit.
   - Be sensitive to the leadership of the Holy Spirit.
   - Love God and love people.

3. Enlist an apprentice. Pray about someone who will go through the study as a participant, but who wants to facilitate a group in the future.

4. Consider the skills for leading the group:
   - Be a good communicator.
   - Be a good listener.
   - Be an encourager.
   - Know how to keep one person from dominating the group.
   - Know how to involve members in the discussion.
   - Be a servant leader.

5. Identify foundational concepts for the group:
   - Group members will be asked to make a commitment to attend all sessions.
   - Group members will be asked to sign a covenant.
   - Group members will maintain confidentiality with each other.
   - All sessions will begin and end on time.
   - Group members will agree to pray for one another regularly.
   - Group members will faithfully participate in each session.
   - A safe environment will permeate at all sessions.

6. Arrange for a location in either a home or other facility.

7. Order any necessary materials from The Center for Faithwalk Leadership or from your local Christian bookstore. See the resource section in the back of this Leader's Guide.

Preparation Guidelines for the Group Leader

As you prepare for your role as group leader remember the following principles for leading a group study:

1. Review session goals for each week's study.

2. Approach each group session in prayer and humility.

A. Ask the Holy Spirit for guidance. What issues are most important right now for the people in your group? In this way you are preparing for people, not merely preparing for a meeting. This will help you keep your focus on the task. The group's purpose is for members to encounter God's truth, and by the Holy Spirit's work and grace, have that truth illuminated to them in their life situations as leaders. Ask God for guidance as you serve your group members.

B. It is essential that you resist the pressure to "produce a good meeting" or preserve your reputation. Your preparation should be for the purpose of pleasing God and serving the members of your group. God should be honored in each of your group meetings.

C. If you are overly concerned about how you will do or how the meeting will go, your focus is on yourself rather than pleasing God. Remember, your group meetings are "not about you;" they are about helping others learn to Lead Like Jesus.

D. Don't just remember what Jesus said, but believe it, "Remain in Me, and I will remain in you. No branch can bear fruit by itself; it must remain in the vine. Neither can you bear fruit unless you remain in Me" (John 15:4).

3. Provide an atmosphere for comfortable discussions.

A. Create an environment where everyone is free to ask questions.

B. Create an atmosphere of respect. Practice active listening—listening attentively to others, looking at them, nodding your head, paying attention. Listening and showing respect will help cultivate trust among group members.

C. Work to draw questions from the responses of the group. Do they understand the issue being discussed? Are they seeing it for the first time? Are they sensing conviction? How you respond to their comments either will facilitate the Spirit's work or hinder it.

D. Create an atmosphere that is not distracting:

- Make sure the room has adequate light and comfortable seating.

- Cell phones and pagers are turned off.

- Make sure the room is neat and clean.

4. Understand and apply God's Word.

A. Review all Scripture used in each week's study.

B. Memorize the assigned verse for each week.

C. Watch all Visual Bible segments prior to each group session.

D. Consider what the truths taught in each session mean to you here and now. How does knowing this truth about God make a difference in your life?

E. How can you apply this truth?

- What are the implications to you and to your group members?

- Is there a command in this passage that leaders are required to obey?

- *Is there an example to follow?*

F. *What does this truth tell you about people in general? How does this apply to you and your group members? Now that you have learned these things what can you do to help others walk in obedience?*

5. Be sensitive to the Holy Spirit.

   A. *Pray for and expect the Holy Spirit's help in leading the group session each week.*

   B. *Be open to His leadership as your group meets and discusses key issues that relate to leading like Jesus.*

   C. *Ask God to help you begin to model leading like Jesus in all areas of your life as you lead this group study.*

*Some of the information above was adapted from *Leading Effective Discussions Guide*, Kenneth Maresco, Sovereign Grace Ministries

How to Use This Leader's Guide

Each Group Session plan includes three parts:

1. Pre-Session—This section includes administrative tasks for you to complete as group members are arriving and getting settled. Tasks include providing name tags, registration forms, appropriate music or other media that coordinates with the theme of the week, and "Personal Concerns" forms where group members can note their needs, prayer requests, and the like.

2. Session—This section offers learning activities for you to use in conducting a ninety-minute group session. The activities follow a similar pattern each week. Learning activities will be based on the EXP Transformational Model.*

EXPand Truth Application
Group members will discuss truths that were revealed to them during the previous week's study.

EXPect Transformation
Group members will probe how previous sessions impacted the members' thoughts or perspectives about a particular topic.

EXPose Concerns
You'll help uncover objections that group members might have regarding the concepts they have been studying.

EXPlore Content
At this point the leader should focus the group's attention on the content from that week's individual study, sharing of personal experiences, and responses to that content.

EXPlain Concepts
Help group members take truth into their hearts and minds by having them explain the concepts they have been studying.

EXPress Confirmation
Your group will discuss the changes that could occur in the learner's attitude.

EXPerience Conformation
Behavioral changes that will occur as a result of your study will be examined.

3. Planning for the Future—This section of the group session plan helps you evaluate the group session, analyze your performance as a leader, identify ways to better serve the needs of the group, and encourage participation from each group member. Your early sensitivity to group members who dominate discussion and those who are reluctant to speak can do wonders in maintaining group commitment and enthusiasm.

*Leaders can obtain detailed information on the EXP Transformational Model on page 14 of this Leader's Guide and on the DVD with the Group Leader Session Overviews.

Group Leader Video Resources

*Lead Like Jesus:
Beginning the Journey
Group Study Video Segments*

The group study video segments are for use during the weekly group sessions. They are optional, but because the content in these videos is rich, please try to allow enough time during the session to show the clips.

Lead Like Jesus DVD #1

For Introductory Session and Study Guide Sessions 1-4

Video Segment 1: Ken Blanchard's Personal Testimony

Video Segment 2: The Visual Bible–Matthew 20:20-28

Video Segment 3: The Heart–The EGO Diagram (Phil Hodges)

Video Segment 4: The Visual Bible–Matthew 3:1-4:11

Video Segment 5: Self Serving vs. Servant Leaders (Ken Blanchard)

Video Segment 6: The Heart and Exalting God Only (Phil Hodges)

Video Segment 7: The Head–First Role of Leadership: Vision (Ken Blanchard)

Video Segment 8: The Head–The Second Role of Leadership: Implementation (Ken Blanchard)

Lead Like Jesus DVD #2

For Study Guide Sessions 5-8

Video Segment 9: The Hands–Jesus: A Situational Leader (Ken Blanchard)

Video Segment 10: D1–The Visual Bible–Matthew 4:18-22

Video Segment 11: D2–The Visual Bible–Matthew 17:15-18

Video Segment 12: D3–The Visual Bible–Matthew 14:22-23

Video Segment 13: D4–The Visual Bible–Acts 2:36-47

Video Segment 14: S1–The Visual Bible–Matthew 10:5-10

Video Segment 15: S2–The Visual Bible–Matthew 17:18-20

Video Segment 16: S3–The Visual Bible–Matthew 14:22-33

Video Segment 17: S4–The Visual Bible–Matthew 28:18-20

Video Segment 18: The Habits–Solitude (Phil Hodges)

Video Segment 19: The Habits–Unconditional Love (Phil Hodges)

Video Segment 20: The Habits–Accountability Relationships (Ken Blanchard)

Video Segment 21: The One Minute Apology (Ken Blanchard)

Video Segment 22: Closing Words (Ken Blanchard)

Lead Like Jesus DVD #3

Group Leader Session Overviews (Lee Ross and Avery Willis)

This video is for the group leader to use as a resource in preparing for each week of the study. Each of the eleven segments will include important information for the group leader as he or she plans each group session.

(For use w/ Book Club)

LEAD LIKE JESUS: EXP LEARNING MODEL™

The EXP Learning Model™
The Process of
Transformational Learning

We learn what we need to know . . . to survive . . . to prosper . . . to satisfy expectations, our own or someone else's . . . to succeed . . . to realize destiny. Behind learning there is always a motive. According to Abraham Maslow and others, motivation is intrinsic . . . from inside a person. Motivation is a matter of the heart and the head. In the purest sense of the word, we cannot motivate anyone. We can, however, stimulate motivation within them.

Our world is becoming increasingly more frenzied. Attention spans are measured in sound bites and fed with cyber bytes. Our theories and methods, which have driven the teaching–learning process of the Twentieth Century and before, are proving inadequate. The end goal of learning always has implied some kind of change in the learner's knowledge, attitude, or behavior. Is learning even learning if it doesn't affect these domains within a person? Learning means change.

READ ALOUD
The most potent learning is transformational. In Christian growth, we are admonished that we be transformed by the renewing of our minds (Romans 12:2). Ultimately, that transformational process encompasses the whole of life. Transformational leadership grows out of transformational learning. Given all of the mind–dulling distractions that routinely divert our attention from the teaching–learning process, what are we to do? How can we learn? How can we teach so that others can learn?

One thing is for certain in Twenty–first Century educational methodology: attention spans are indeed shorter than ever and getting shorter by the moment. Any attempt at helping learners learn—whatever their age—has to take this into account. Thus, the EXP Learning Model™!

The EXP Learning Model™ assumes that serious learners approach opportunities for learning with a "transformational **expectation**": *What difference will this make*? That difference may be noble or practical or personal or anything else. Regardless of where it stands on the scale of ultimate significance and impact, the would–be learner approaches a learning opportunity looking through the process

14

to the other side with a mixture of suspicion, wonderment, anxiety, resistance, and a thousand other attitudes. Too often, learning opportunities are reduced to learning options! Yet, given a clear vision of just what the transformational potential or value of the learning process might prove to be, the learner ventures beyond expectation to **exposing his/her concerns:** *What might this transformation cost me? How might it change me? How might it . . . ?* Learning hangs on overcoming objections, because learning implies change and change produces resistance.

As concerns are exposed and addressed honestly, the learner is willing to venture into **exploring content**. Digging into the facts and figures, the bits and bytes, the jots and tittles of . . . TRUTH! As learners are brought into the presence of truth (whatever form it takes) their resistance to truth's transforming power is reduced, and they begin to grasp personal implications and **explain concepts**. They understand. Cognitive learning has taken root. Knowledge is gleaned and gained. Transformational learning implies an increase in one's working knowledge.

Close behind explaining concepts follows **expressing confirmation**. *What will I do with this new–found truth? How will it affect my attitude . . . the way I think and feel? Will I allow it to work its life–changing potential in my heart and mind?* Transformational learning produces attitudinal change, especially when "truth" is the transforming Truth of Christ!

Ultimately, though, transformational learning reaches its full meaning and measure as it is lived out in **experiencing conformation**. For the Christian, this is that process of so–called sanctification, that continuous changing of a person's core being from one degree to another into the likeness of Christ . . . *being conformed to His image*! In traditional learning, too much of the time the intent was to produce conformity to some human–defined standard. In transformational learning, however, the intent is *always* to produce conformation to the notion and nature of Jesus of Nazareth,

The EXP Learning Model™

EXPectation → { EXPosure, EXPloration, EXPlanation } → EXPression > EXPerience

The EXP Learning Model™ was conceived and developed by Jesse G. Palmer in association with the *Lead Like Jesus* Movement and Faithwalk Leadership. All rights reserved. Copyright 2003.

15

the living Lord and Savior.

In the EXP Learning Model™, we should always be clear with our motives as we appeal to the motives of those we seek to teach: *our goal is that believers be transformed into leaders who lead like Jesus. That should be their expectation as they stand on the precipice of a leadership–changing learning encounter with Jesus of Nazareth.*

Scripture Memory Cards

Week 1
"Not so with you. Instead, whoever wants to become great among you must be your servant." (Matthew 20:26)

Week 2
"May the words of my mouth and the meditations of my heart be pleasing in Your sight, O LORD, my Rock and my Redeemer." (Psalm 19:14)

Week 3
"He must increase, but I must decrease." (John 3:30)

Week 4
"Do not conform any longer to the pattern of this world, but be transformed by the renewing of your mind. Then you will be able to test and approve what God's will is—His good, pleasing and perfect will." (Romans 12:2)

Week 5
"Come follow Me," Jesus said, "and I will make you fishers of men." (Matthew 4:19)

Week 6
"But his delight is in the law of the LORD, and on his law he meditates day and night. He is like a tree planted by streams of water, which yields its fruit in season and whose leaf does not wither. Whatever he does prospers. (Psalm 1:2–3)

Week 7
"Do not merely listen to the word, and so deceive yourselves. Do what it says." (James 1:22)

Week 8
"Now that you know these things, you will be blessed if you do them." (John 13:17)

As group leader, you have permission to make copies of this page to hand out at your group sessions.

Personal Concerns

Use this page to keep a record of prayer concerns for the group. Name, Prayer Requests, Needs, Concerns, Questions, etc.

As group leader, you have permission to make copies of this page to pass around at your group sessions.

LEAD LIKE JESUS: INTRODUCTORY SESSION

THURS (Session One)

Conduct this Introductory Session before your group members study Week One of Lead Like Jesus.

SESSION GOALS

By the end of this session, members will be able to demonstrate their commitment to *Lead Like Jesus* by . . .

- Telling at least one new fact about each member.
- Explaining the "Not So with You" mandate. *ASK WHAT THIS PHRASE MEANS*
- Describing the four dimensions of leading Like Jesus.
- Agreeing to complete the first week's materials.
- Signing a group covenant.

CENTRAL TRUTH:

 Jesus calls those who follow Him to lead differently.

PRE—SESSION:

Select and play appropriate music. Greet everyone as they arrive and make nametags.

SESSION

Introduction (10-15 minutes)

1. Welcome each person and point them to the refreshments (if they will be served at the beginning). Ask everyone to prepare and wear a nametag. As members arrive, introduce each one to others in the room. Let everyone visit informally until it is time to begin.

2. Begin promptly. Remind the group that you will begin and end each session on time. Group members may fellowship before and after each session, but they can depend on you to be prompt.

3. Thank each participant for coming to this opening session of the *Lead Like Jesus* Study Group.

4. Ask each member to share one fact about themselves that members of the group might not know and give a brief statement about why they are interested in learning to *Lead Like Jesus*.

5. Offer a prayer of thanksgiving to God for bringing you together to learn how to glorify Him by learning to *Lead Like Jesus*. Ask the Holy Spirit to be your Teacher

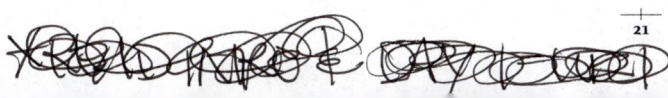

during the session. Ask Him to begin bonding your lives together in Christian love and unity during the sessions of this study.

Part One: Overview of Lead Like Jesus (30-40 minutes)

1. Say in your own words... I want to thank you for coming to this introductory session of the *Lead Like Jesus* Group Study. In the next thirty minutes I want to tell you four things:

- How the Lead like Jesus message applies to you and what you do every day.
- What Jesus calls those who follow Him to do differently as leaders.
- Why I am excited about the Lead Like Jesus Group Study.
- How the Group study works and what it will require to participate.
- Review the steps for making this a transformational experience, page 14 of this Leader's Guide.

2. Have group members turn to Week One, Day One in their study guides and follow along as you read the statements just under the introduction.

- Ask group members what they think when they hear: "Business and Belief"?
- Ask group members what they think when they hear: "Jesus and Your Job"?
- Ask group members what they think when they hear: "Personal and Professional"?
- Ask group members what they think when they hear: "Servant and Leader"?
- Ask group members why they think some people feel uneasy when they see these words grouped together?

3. Say... To give you a brief overview of the purpose behind the *Lead Like Jesus* group study I am going to show you a video clip featuring Ken Blanchard, the co–author of this study. Ken has authored more than 31 books, including *The One Minute Manager®*, *Leadership By the Book*, *The Servant Leader*, *Whale Done!™*, *Raving Fans®*, *Gung Ho!®*, and *The One Minute Apology™*. Ken is also co–founder of the Center for Faithwalk Leadership that is dedicated to "Challenging and Equipping people to *Lead Like Jesus*."

4. Show... LLJ Video Segment 1—Ken Blanchard's Personal Testimony (14:00)

5. Ask the Group... What are some reasons why you think Jesus has been overlooked as a practical leadership role model? (Possible responses—"Because of who He is." "The Son of God." "Too far removed from the issues of leading today." "Too controversial to bring up in a non–ministry situation.")

6. Ask the Group... How do you think the leadership in the organization or group you serve in would be different if Jesus of Nazareth was the number one role model?

7. Say... Let me ask you a question. "How many of you consider yourselves leaders? Raise your hand."

- If everyone raises their hand, skip to point #9.
- If some hands are not raised, continue on with point #8:

8. Say... Now I am going to give you our definition of leadership and then ask you the same question again. We define leadership as "Any time you are seeking to influence the thinking behavior of another person." I will repeat it. "Leadership is any time you are seeking to influence the thinking or behavior of another person." Now using that definition of leadership, how many of you consider yourselves as engaging in leadership on a daily basis? Raise your hand.

9. Say... The fact of the matter is that we all take on the role of leader in all of our relationships when we try and influence the thoughts and actions of other people. Sometimes leadership takes on an official role in an organization such as Manager, Teacher, Pastor, or Coach. Sometimes it takes place in relationship defined by the structure of a family—Father and Mother, Husband and Wife, Brother and Sister, Son and Daughter. Sometimes it takes place in voluntary relationships like Friend and Teammate, and Volunteer.

At this point have participants share which of their daily leadership roles is most important to them. Give the group about two minutes before resuming the discussion.

10. Say... In each these relationships, we engage in hundreds of acts of leadership on a daily basis. When we do we are faced with the same choice—either to serve our own self-interest as our primary goal or serve the best interests of the other person.

- A basic question for each of us to answer is—How does the fact that I am a follower of Jesus make a difference in the way I treat my leadership opportunities?
- What we are here for is to take a new look at how to lead while we seek to follow Jesus.
- Explain the Jesus Transformational Journey Model (p.14) so they can see how the overview of this course will help them in various levels.

★ SHOW POWERPOINT EXP

Part 2: Overview of the Lead Like Jesus Study (35-50 Minutes)

1. Say... Look at the diagram on page 15. Over the next eight weeks, we will be looking into four specific dimensions of leadership to learn what it means to *Lead Like Jesus*:

- The Heart or motivations of leadership

- The Head or assumptions about the role of the leader
- The Hands or behaviors of a leader
- And the Habits or the daily ways for a leader to stay on course

Each week we'll explore one or more of these dimensions.

- Week One of the study will cover some of the foundational concepts of Leading like Jesus in an Overview Format which should be completed before our next meeting
- Weeks Two covers The Heart–Transforming Your Leadership Intentions and Motivation
- Week Three covers The Heart, part II–Exalting God Only
- Week Four covers The Head or Assumptions of a Leader
- Week Five covers The Hand or Leadership Behavior
- Week Six covers The Habits of the Leader
- Week Seven covers Leadership Skills
- Week Eight covers Next Steps for Walking the Talk of Leading Like Jesus

2. Say . . . This course is designed to combine individual study and group learning experiences in order to create a sound foundation for real and lasting change in the ways we lead and represent Jesus in the world around us. It will require both a degree of personal discipline to make the daily learning experiences a priority and a commitment to serve the growth and development of the group through regular attendance. If you are unsure whether you would be willing to make a commitment to complete the entire *Lead Like Jesus* Study, including making weekly attendance at the group meeting a priority, please let me know before next week's meeting. If you are willing to make a commitment tonight, please fill out the *Lead Like Jesus* Group Study Commitment Form you will find in your Study Guide.

3. Tell them the expected outcomes of completing the course.

4. Ask if there are any questions and concerns.

5. Announce the next week's meeting with time and place and hosting responsibilities assigned.

6. Close in prayer for the upcoming weeks as the group begins the journey of learning what it means to Lead Like Jesus.

Planning for the Future — After the Session

Pray specifically for each member before the next group session.

Call all members and encourage them as they study the Week One material. Thank them for their commitment to the group.

Use the following questions to evaluate your leadership:

- *Was I prepared?*
- *Was my presentation clear?*
- *Did I follow the Leader's Guide?*
- *Did I provide positive leadership?*
- *Was I a servant leader?*
- *Did I create a positive group environment?*
- *Did I help members communicate with each other?*
- *Do the members understand the purpose of the study?*

Read "Personal Preparation before the Session" on page 7 for the next group session to evaluate how much preparation you will need.

Carefully study Week One and do all the exercises in your individual Study Guide in order to experience it fully with other members during the next meeting.

LEAD LIKE JESUS: THE BIG PICTURE

THURS (Session Two – Study Guide Week One)

SESSION GOALS

Members supporting one another in understanding the Heart, Head, Hands, and Habits and why leading like Jesus is important to their own walk of faith by . . .

- *Their ability to describe the four dimensions of leadership and the "Not So with You" mandate.*
- *Their willingness to share their greatest leadership challenges.*
- *Their completion of the first week's study and the sharing of their "Aha moments" and best practices.*

CENTRAL TRUTH

→ Jesus IS the perfect leadership model.

PRE—SESSION

Select and play appropriate music. Provide Personal Concerns List.

SESSION

Introduction (15 Minutes)

1. Begin session with prayer and welcome group members.

2. Thank group members for affirming their commitment to the group and the Lead Like Jesus study by signing the commitment form and returning for today's session.

3. Ask members to pair off and recite the memory verse for this week.

Note: Don't expect every participant to have had the same level of positive experience. If questions or negative comments come up, relax and try not to become defensive. Listen for understanding and feel free to say "I don't know" and refer the question to the rest of the group for any insights they might have. When an issue involving the program materials comes up that you can't handle, tell the person you will make note of it and commit to try to find a suitable answer by the next meeting.

EXPand Truth Application

Say . . . Bible study is going to be an important part of our study of Jesus as the greatest leadership role model for all time. As we examine the Scriptures we will occasionally see how *The Visual Bible* interprets the intentions and actions of Jesus.

(*The Visual Bible* is a visual representation of the New International Version of the Bible. It is important to remember that although the only words spoken are Scripture, the actions of the actors are interpretation.)

Show . . . LLJ Video Segment 2—The Visual Bible—Matthew 20:20–28 (3:00)

Ask the Group . . .

- What are some of the leadership lessons we can learn from both the Scripture and the actions of Jesus as portrayed in this video?

- What do you think the "Not So with You" message that Jesus gave to His disciples says to us about the way we lead?

(You will want to emphasize here that Jesus was introducing a new paradigm for leadership for His disciples. Ask the group to share some of the traditional paradigms we have concerning leadership.)

EXPect Transformation

Begin by asking participants the questions listed below. Ask that responses be short and to the point. Pursue one or two responses that have the greatest likelihood of stimulating thought and learning. Remember that there are no right or wrong answers!

Ask the Group . . .

- What did you like most in the first week of study?

- What most impacted you in this week's study?

- Did you encounter any problems in the study?

- What study times and places worked best? How long did your study take?

- What was the most meaningful sentence or Bible verse from this week?

- Ask members to sign the commitment form and pass their books around so everyone can sign. Say, "This will give you a list of all group members and can be a prayer list for you."

EXPose Concerns

Uncover objections that group members might have regarding the concepts they have been studying. The following questions will help surface and overcome those objections. Pursue those that have the greatest relevance to your group.

Ask the Group . . . .

- How does giving God free reign in all your daily actions and relationships relate to your home and office? Is it the same or different?

- What will be the most difficult concept that you studied this week to implement in your life and why?

EXPlore Content

Encourage group members to explore honestly and openly the wealth and scope of content presented to them during the Week One readings. Also encourage them to use their Study Guides to maximize their exploration.

1. Why is it important to understand the four dimensions of leadership?
2. What role does your "Heart" play in leadership decisions?
3. What role does your "Head" assume in your leadership role?
4. What role does your "Hands" address in your leadership?
5. How do your "Habits" affect your leadership responsibilities?

EXPress Confirmation

In groups of three, consider the following thoughts:

- Describe a life designed to please yourself and then a life designed to please God.
- Share a time when God changed your perspective from your purpose to His.
- What are the results when trust is missing? When trust is present?
- Share your answer to the question, "Are you a self-serving or a servant leader?" which you answered on Day Four of this week's study.

EXPlain Concepts

Help group members take truth into their hearts and minds by having them explain concepts that they have been studying. Remember that the more accurate and comfortable they are in explaining these concepts succinctly in their own words, the more they have understood the truth, and the more likely they are to apply it to their lives.

Say ... Next we are going to take the first step of learning to *Lead Like Jesus* by briefly reviewing the *Lead Like Jesus* Transformational model that you examined this week.

Divide the group into four equal subgroups. Assign each group one element of the *Lead Like Jesus* Transformational Model.

Group 1–Personal Leadership

Group 2–One on One Leadership

Group 3–Team Leadership

Group 4–Organizational Leadership

Each group will meet for ten minutes and develop a five-minute presentation on the key elements of the topics. As each group makes their presentation, stop them exactly on time with some kind of signal, such as a bell, buzzer or whistle. Applaud each group's presentation and ask the whole group if they would add any additional thoughts.

EXPerience Conformation

Ask group members to engage in the following activity during the coming week and report back in the next meeting on their experiences:

- *Share the Transformational Leadership Model with your fellow workers or family and get their feedback. Listen to the comments and record your findings.*

Ask the group if there are any questions or comments.

Ask the group to pray a one-sentence prayer requesting God to open up their hearts and minds for the challenges that lie ahead. If anyone feels uncomfortable praying out loud, they may pray silently.

PLANNING FOR THE FUTURE — AFTER THE SESSION

Pray specifically for each member before the next group session.

Call all members and encourage them in the study of the Week Two material.

Have an answer for any program questions that came up at today's meeting, and if appropriate contact the individual who asked it or wait until the next group meeting.

Use the following questions to evaluate your leadership:

- *Was I prepared?*
- *Was my presentation clear?*
- *Did I follow the Leader's Guide?*
- *Did I provide positive leadership?*
- *Was I a servant leader?*
- *Did I create a positive group environment?*
- *Did I help members communicate with each other?*
- *Do the members understand the purpose of the study?*

Read "Personal Preparation before the Session" for the next group session to evaluate how much preparation you will need.

Carefully study Week Two and do all the exercises in the participant's workbook in order to fully experience it with other group members during the next meeting.

LEAD LIKE JESUS: THE HEART

[Session Three — Study Guide Week Two]

THIRD

★ READ WEEK 2

SESSION GOALS

Group members will support each other by learning to . . .

- *Assess their Servant Leader vs. Self-Serving Leader motivations.*
- *Recognize when they are Edging God Out.*
- *Commit to the EGO's Anonymous 12 Step Process.*
- *Understand the EGO diagram.*

CENTRAL TRUTH

Being a Servant Leader is the highest calling of a believer.

PRE—SESSION

Select and play appropriate music. Provide Personal Concerns List.

SESSION

Introduction (15 Minutes)

1. Begin session with prayer and welcome group members.

2. Thank group members for their continued participation in the Lead Like Jesus study.

3. Ask for volunteers to share one experience from the previous week's EXPerience Conformation assignment. Pursue any experiences that have unusual teaching/learning potential.

4. Pair the group up to recite their memory verse to each other.

EXPand Truth Application

Ask group members to share with one other person in the group (preferably not their spouse) their reaction to the EGO (Edging God Out) diagram and how it related to them personally.

EXPect Transformation

Begin by asking participants the questions below. Ask that responses be short and to the point. Pursue one or two that have the greatest likelihood of stimulating thought and learning. Remember that there are no right or wrong answers!

- *What one thing did you learn in this week's study that you did not know before?*
- *Based on your study, what is one area of personal growth you identified?*

READ DAY

EXPose Concerns

Uncover objections that group members might have regarding the concepts they have been studying. The following questions will help surface and overcome those objections. Pursue those that have the greatest relevance to your group.

Ask the Group . . .

- *Do you feel that the words "servant leader" are overused or misunderstood today? If yes, what other terminology would you use to express these concepts?*
- *What is the value of feedback at home or is it a business concept only?*
- *Can you Edge God Out at work and not at home and still be a servant leader or vice versa?*

EXPlore Content

Show . . . LLJ Video Segment 3—The Heart —The EGO Diagram (Phil Hodges, 8:50)

Refer group members to the EGO Diagram as you review the concepts about fear and pride:

- *Always separates—man from God, from other people, and from himself/herself.*
- *Always compares—with others and is never happy.*
- *Always distorts—the truth into a false sense of security or fear.*

Ask the Group . . . Does this diagram make sense to you? If yes, in what way? Would you add or subtract anything from it? If it doesn't make sense, how would you change it? What would you add or subtract?

Review the three statements about how we Edge God Out:

1. *We edge God out when we put something else in God's place as the object of our worship.*
2. *We edge God out when we rely on other sources for our security and sufficiency.*
3. *We edge God out when we put others in His place as our major audience.*

Ask the Group . . .

- *What are other objects of worship? (Answers may include job, prestige, TV, relationships, etc.)*
- *How do you edge God out? How does the edging God out happen? (All at once, over time, etc.)*
- *What are other sources for our security and sufficiency? (Answers may include job, finances, health, etc.) Why do we think these things are important? How long will they last? What can remove them?*
- *How do we put others in God's place as our major audience? Who do we put as our audience? (Answers may include managers, supervisors, parents, spouse, children, etc.)*
- *How can we put God back in His rightful place as our major audience? What will that do to our other relationships?*

Show . . . LLJ Video Segment 4—The Visual Bible—Matthew 3:1–4:11 **PRE PREP**

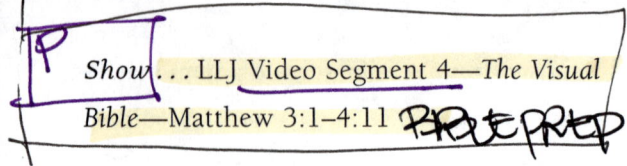

Ask the Group . . .

- *What is the main point of the encounter in the video segment we just watched?*
- *What were the temptations that Jesus faced?*
- *How did Jesus refute the tempter each time? What was the tool He used?*
- *How did Jesus demonstrate His heart in each segment of this story?*

EXPlain Concepts

Help group members take truth into their hearts and minds by having them explain concepts that they have been studying. Remember that the more accurate and comfortable they are in explaining these concepts succinctly in their own words, the more they have understood the truth and the more likely they are to apply it to their lives.

Divide the group into teams of three and ask them discuss their responses to the five tests found in the past week's material. Allow 15 minutes for this exercise.

Bring the groups back together and ask for volunteers to share their thoughts, feelings, and comments about the exercises. Where did they rate themselves? Were there any surprises? Did it confirm what you already suspected? What did you learn about yourself and others?

EXPress Confirmation

In groups of three, discuss the following:

- *How successful have you been at personal succession planning? Why or why not?*
- *What is your greatest fear and why?*

EXPerience Conformation **HANDOUT 12 STEP ← HERE**

Draw the group together and tell them we are going to participate in a short exercise similar to an Alcoholics Anonymous meeting, except that this meeting will be called EGO's Anonymous. Remind them of the EGO diagram and the fact that we are addicted to SELF. Give these directions:

1. As group members feel comfortable ask them to stand and say "Hi, my name is _____ and I have an EGO problem." To which the group responds, "Hi (__insert name of person__)!"

2. The person standing says, "I have an EGO problem because_____."

3. The person may then be seated. Each person is allowed time to participate. When a reasonable amount of time has passed, bring the experience to a close.

Ask the Group . . .

- *How did you feel during this activity? Why?*
- *Did anyone find this activity difficult or uncomfortable? Why?*
- *Why would we conduct an activity like this in a study on leadership?*

Pass out the copies you made of the "EGO's Anonymous 12–Step Process." Review and discuss several of the steps listed.

Note to Group Leader: LLJ Video Segment 5—The Heart—Self Serving vs. Servant Leaders (Ken Blanchard, 6:15), is an excellent resource for additional discussion on the difference between a servant leader and a self–serving leader.

PLANNING FOR THE FUTURE — AFTER THE SESSION

Before the next group session pray specifically for each member

Call all members and encourage them in their ongoing study of the Week Two material.

Have an answer for any program questions that came up at the meeting, and if appropriate contact the individual who asked it or wait until the next group meeting.

Use the following questions to evaluate your leadership:

- *Was I prepared?*
- *Was my presentation clear?*
- *Did I follow the leader guide?*
- *Did I provide positive leadership?*
- *Was I a servant leader?*
- *Did I create a positive group environment?*
- *Did I help members communicate with each other?*
- *Do the members understand the purpose of the study?*

Read "Personal Preparation before the Session" on page 7 for the next group session to evaluate how much preparation you will need.

Carefully study Week Three and do all the exercises in the participant's workbook in order to experience it fully with other members during the next meeting.

DISCUSS ANSWERS IN WB

LEAD LIKE JESUS: EXALTING GOD ONLY

(Session Four — Study Guide Week Three)

SESSION GOALS

Group members will support each other by learning to . . .

- *Recognize the characteristics of a Servant Leader.*
- *Exalt God Only.*
- *Altar—not merely alter—their EGO.*
- *Understand the EGO diagram.*

CENTRAL TRUTH

All aspects of a believer's life are dependent on and flow from a personal relationship with God.

PRE—SESSION

Select and play appropriate music. Provide Personal Concerns List.

SESSION

Introduction (15 Minutes)

1. Begin session with prayer and welcome group members.

2. Read the EGO's Anonymous 12–Step Process in unison.

3. Ask for volunteers to share one experience from the previous week's EXPerience Conformation assignment. Pursue any experiences that have unusual teaching/learning potential.

4. Pair the group to recite their memory verse to each other.

EXPand Truth Application

Ask your group members to share their reactions to the EGO's Anonymous activity at the end of the last group session.

Ask the Group . . . Do you agree that you are an egomaniac? Why or why not?

EXPect Transformation

Begin by asking participants the questions listed below. Ask that responses be short and to the point. Pursue one or two that have the greatest likelihood of stimulating thought and learning. Remember that there are no right or wrong answers!

Ask the Group . . . Which statements of the EGO's Anonymous 12–Step Process do you most agree with?

- *What comes to your mind first when you*

hear the word "worship"?

- *How has the content of the Week One and Week Two lessons impacted your life?*
- *What one sentence or Bible verse meant the most to you this week?*

EXPose Concerns

Uncover objections that group members might have about the concepts they have been studying. The following questions will help surface and overcome those objections. Pursue those that have the greatest relevance to your group.

Ask the Group . . .

- *What is your first thought when change is introduced?*
- *What does "total surrender" mean to you, and how will it impact your life personally and professionally? What are the consequences of less-than-total surrender?*
- *Consider the word "servant"—what picture comes to your mind?*

EXPlore Content

Encourage group members to explore honestly and openly the wealth and scope of content presented to them as they went through Week Three of the Study Guide. Also encourage them to use their workbooks to maximize their exploration.

Ask the Group . . .

- *What does it mean to worship God with your whole heart? How do you do this?*
- *How did Jesus depend on God completely as His source? How should we depend on God completely?*
- *Do you ever have problems with focusing on people as your audience? What can help us focus on God as the audience? (Be sure that they mention worshipping God only.)*

Show . . . LLJ Video Segment 6: The Heart and Exalting God Only with Phil Hodges (5:20)

Ask the Group . . .

- *What picture does the term "servant" cause to come to your mind?*
- *What answers did you put to the questions about how you could follow Jesus' example as a servant leader? (Phil. 2:1-9)*
- *How did you respond to the rights the servant must give up? (Luke 17:7-10)*
- *What did God say to you in Day 3 about being a servant?*

Refer group members to the EGO diagram as you review the following concepts about humility and confidence:

- *Truth Instead of Distortion as a basis for Decision Making*
- *Transparent Relationships Instead of Isolation*

- Community Instead of Destructive Competition

Ask the Group . . .

- Does the EGO diagram make sense to you?
- If yes, in what way? Would you add or subtract anything from it?
- If it doesn't make sense, how would you change it? What would you add or subtract?

GET BIBLE READY.

Review the first four commandments from Exodus 20:3–8 and ask group members to share as many modern applications as possible for each one. Allow time to worship God at the conclusion of the sharing time.

Read Psalm 139:1–12 and *Ask the Group* the following questions:

- How does it feel to know that God is aware of every aspect of your life?
- What else does God do besides know you? What does this tell you about God?
- What are attributes of God are implied in this psalm?
- What relationship is pictured in verse 10? In what ways do people try to escape from the knowledge and presence of God? How successful are these attempts?

EXPlain Concepts

Help group members take truth into their hearts and minds by having them explain concepts that they have been studying. Remember that the more accurate and comfortable they are in explaining these concepts succinctly in their own words, the more they have understood the truth and the more likely they are to apply it to their lives.

Divide the group in half. Ask one group to prepare a 5–minute presentation on humility as described in the EGO (Exalting God Only) diagram, and ask the other group to prepare a 5–minute presentation on confidence as described in the Exalting God Only diagram. After 10 minutes, ask the groups to report. After each report, invite the other group to contribute to the work of the presenting group or to ask questions for clarity.

EXPress Confirmation

Invite members to read in unison the first six steps of the "EGO's Anonymous 12–Step Process." Ask group members to pair up and to discuss their understanding of each of these six steps. Call the participants back to the large group, and ask group members to affirm these six steps and to acknowledge them as their commitment in the group study.

EXPerience Conformation

Ask group members to engage in one of the following activities during the coming week and report back in the next meeting on their experiences:

Read the "EGO's Anonymous 12-Step Process" every day until next week's group session. Pray through the first six steps and record any insights.

Choose an activity that demonstrates a servant heart and humility, and perform that act of service before the next session. Answer the following questions about your experience:

- *What did I do to show a servant heart?*
- *What was the reaction of the people I attempted to serve?*
- *How was I blessed by serving these people?*
- *Would I do this activity again? If not, why not or what would you need to change?*

Planning for the Future — After the Session

Pray specifically for each member before the next group session.

Call all members and encourage them in their ongoing study and application of the Week Three material.

Answer any program questions that came up at today's meeting, and if appropriate contact the individual who asked the question or wait until the next group meeting.

Use the following questions to evaluate your leadership:

- *Was I prepared?*
- *Was my presentation clear?*
- *Did I follow the Leader's Guide?*
- *Did I provide positive leadership?*
- *Was I a servant leader?*
- *Did I create a positive group environment?*
- *Did I help members communicate with each other?*
- *Do the members understand the purpose of the study?*

Read "Personal Preparation before the Session" before the next group session to evaluate how much preparation you will need.

Carefully study Week Four and do all the exercises in the participant's workbook in order to experience it fully with other group members during the next meeting.

LEAD LIKE JESUS: THE HEAD

(Session Five – Study Guide Week Four)

SESSION GOALS

Group members will support each other by learning to . . .

- *Identify their own values and why those values are important.*
- *Write a personal mission statement.*
- *Develop a compelling vision.*

CENTRAL TRUTH

Servant Leadership begins with a clear and compelling vision of the future that excites passion and commitment in those who follow.

PRE—SESSION

Select and play appropriate music. Provide Personal Concerns List.

SESSION

Introduction (15 Minutes)

1. Begin session with prayer and welcome group members.

2. Read the "EGO's Anonymous 12–Step Process" in unison.

3. Ask for volunteers to share one experience from the previous week's **EXPerience Conformation** assignment. Pursue any experiences that have unusual teaching/learning potential.

EXPand Truth Application

Pair your group members and ask them to share their two leadership points of view from Day One of Week Four. Ask them to share what changed their perspective, how difficult it was, and how the new point of view will demonstrate their success and effectiveness.

Also, have pairs recite their memory verse for the week to each other.

EXPect Transformation

Begin by asking participants the following questions. Ask that responses be short and to the point. Pursue one or two that have the greatest likelihood of stimulating thought and learning. Remember that there are no right or wrong answers!

Ask the Group . . .

- *How would you summarize your understanding of a servant leader up to this point?*

- What is the key that unlocks your servant leader heart?
- How effective do you believe this model to be?
- What one statement or verse from this lesson most describes your view of servant leadership?

EXPose Concerns

Uncover objections that group members might have regarding the concepts they have been studying. The questions below will help surface and overcome those objections. Pursue those that have the greatest relevance to your group.

Ask the Group...

- Comment on the statement "No organization will rise above the passion of its leader."
- What is the benefit of developing your own purpose/mission statement? What is the result of not having a personal purpose/mission statement?
- Have you considered writing your own obituary? What would you want to include and what would you want to exclude?

EXPlore Content

Encourage group members to explore honestly and openly the wealth and scope of content presented to them during their personal study of Week Four. Also encourage them to use their workbooks to maximize their exploration.

Ask the Group...

- According to the authors, what are the two roles of leadership?
    - A visionary role—doing the right thing the right way.
    - An implementation role—doing things right with a focus on people.
- Why is focusing on long-range effectiveness preferred over short-term success?
- Discuss how long-range effectiveness focuses on accomplishing both the goals and the growth and development of those involved in producing the desired end.

P
Show... LLJ Video Segment 7—The Head—The First Role of Leadership: Vision (Ken Blanchard, 12:00)

Ask the Group... **VALUE CARDS EXERCISE**

- What are the three parts to a compelling vision?
    - Your Purpose—Who you are.
    - Your Picture of the Future—Where you are going.
    - Your Values - What guides your journey.
- What does your personal view of the future look like? What are your personal values?
- Bob Buford, founder of Leadership Network and author, says your personal view of the future should fit on a T-shirt.

What would your T-shirt say?

- How does your employer's vision and values effect you? Do you have any personal concerns related to them?

- Re-read the Seneca quote: "Without a port in mind, any wind will do." What did Seneca mean? What caution does this quote offer us?

- Why is a "picture of the future" valuable to an organization? What was Jesus' picture of the future? What was/is its value to Jesus' followers?

- What suggestions would you make to someone writing organizational values?

- What were Jesus' values? How did they manifest themselves in His life?

- What are some symptoms of an organization with a traditional hierarchical pyramid?

- How did Jesus lead His disciples?

Show . . . LLJ Video Segment 8—The Head—The Second Role of Leadership: Implementation (Ken Blanchard, 8:15)

Ken says that in order to effectively turn the pyramid upside down, you must "raise the development of people to the same level of production."

Ask the Group . . .

- What does Ken's statement mean for the leader who wants to Lead Like Jesus?

- On Day Five of the Week Three study, what were your answers to the questions:

1. How did Jesus facilitate growth and the development of His followers by relinquishing control?

2. How did Jesus make provision for the future well being of His followers?

3. Where did you rate yourself on the scale of 1-10 in giving emphasis to people and task? What was the difference in your answer than when you did it on Day 1?

EXPlain Concepts

Help group members take truth into their hearts and minds by having them explain concepts that they have been studying. Remember that the more accurate and comfortable they are in explaining these concepts succinctly in their own words, the more they have understood the truth and the more likely they are to apply it to their lives.

Divide into groups of three. Ask members to share their personal purpose/mission statement and to explain why they chose the words that they did, what it means to them, and how they would put it on a T-shirt. Ask a spokesperson from each group to share their most unique T-shirt idea.

EXPress Confirmation

Pair up group members to share the following thoughts:

- What is your "picture of the future" vocationally?
- What values shape your relationships?
- What does your personal "picture of the future" look like?
- How has this week's study shaped your vision and values?
- How will you develop the people you lead?

EXPerience Conformation

Ask group members to engage in one of the following activities during the coming week and report back in the next meeting on their experiences:

- Write your values on a note card and carry it in your purse or pocket. Anytime an opportunity or occasion arises for a demonstration of servant leadership, make a note of the details, how you handled it, what you learned, and how it affected you.
- Identify one specific way you will/can live out your vision during the coming week as an evidence of your being a servant leader. Be prepared to share what you did and how it impacted you and others.

In preparation for next week's Group Session, have group members do the following activity together before this session ends. The purpose is to demonstrate what it is like to be on the receiving end of change and to illustrate the Seven Dynamics of Change.

- Have the group stand and get into pairs. Instruct individuals to face their partner and take one minute to observe everything they can about the person. They should NOT talk during this observation time.
- Now have partners turn their backs to each other and make five changes to their own appearances. When changes are complete, have the partners face each other again and see if they can readily identify each other's changes.
- Have partners turn back-to-back again and make five more changes for a total of ten changes. They can then check again to see if they can identify the changes.
- Repeat the activity one more time for a total of fifteen changes.
- Allow members to "undo" the changes and return to their seats.
- Discuss how members felt about this activity. Allow time for them to express their thoughts and for other group members to respond.
- Explain that they will be studying more about the impact of change in their lives during the next week. Encourage them to pay special attention to sections titled Changing the Way You Act and Changing the People You Lead and be prepared to discuss them at the next group meeting.

DISCUSS WORK BOOK

Planning for the Future — After the Session

Pray specifically for each member before the next group session.

Call all members and encourage them in the study of the Week Five material.

Answer any program questions that came up at today's meeting, and if appropriate contact the individual who asked it or wait until the next group meeting.

Use the following questions to evaluate your leadership:

- *Was I prepared?*
- *Was my presentation clear?*
- *Did I follow the Leader's Guide?*
- *Did I provide positive leadership?*
- *Was I a servant leader?*
- *Did I create a positive group environment?*
- *Did I help members communicate with each other?*
- *Do the members understand the purpose of the study?*

Read "Personal Preparation before the Session" for the next group session to evaluate how much preparation you will need.

Carefully study the Week Five material and do all the exercises in the participant's workbook in order to experience it fully with other group members during the next meeting.

LEAD LIKE JESUS: CHANGING YOUR LEADERSHIP BEHAVIOR

(Session Six – Study Guide Week Five)

NOTE TO THE Group Leader: For additional information on the concepts found in *Situational Leadership II®*, you may want to read *Leadership and the One Minute Manager* by Ken Blanchard. This book explains in greater details the key ideas behind *Situational Leadership II®*.

SESSION GOALS

Participants will support each other by learning to:

- *See Jesus as a situational leader*
- *Understand the components of the Situational Leadership Diagram*
- *Recognize the Four Basic Leadership Styles*
- *Embrace change*

CENTRAL TRUTH

Modeling correct behavior is crucial for a servant leader.

PRE—SESSION

Select and play appropriate music. Provide Personal Concerns List.

SESSION

Introduction (15 Minutes)

1. Begin session with prayer and welcome participants.

2. Ask each person to read one of the "EGO's Anonymous 12-Step Process" until all twelve have been read.

3. Ask for volunteers to share one experience from the Week Four EXPerience Conformation assignment. Pursue any experiences that have unusual teaching/learning potential.

4. Pair the group to recite their memory verse to each other.

Show ... LLJ Video Segment 9—The Hands—Jesus: A Situational Leader (Ken Blanchard, 22:10)

EXPand Truth Application

Pair the group and ask each group member to share with their partner the barriers they face in becoming a situational leader, how those barrier might be overcome, and the value of overcoming them.

WATCH VIDEO & HAVE OPEN DISCUSSION

Note to Group Leader... On the enclosed DVD you will find additional video segments from *The Visual Bible* that aid in the understanding of the *Situational Leadership II® Development Levels and Leadership Styles*. Listed below is a rationale for the why the authors thought these video segments might suggest the assigned Development Level or Leadership Style. Please remember as you watch *the Visual Bible* segments that although the words are directly from the Word of God, the actions of the characters are the interpretation of humans.

Say... We're now going to watch several video clips that illustrate Development Levels and Leadership Styles

Show... LLJ Video Segment 10—D1—*The Visual Bible*—Matthew 4:18–22 (2:37)

Rationale: In this segment the disciples are portrayed as individuals who are being called to a new task of becoming fishers of men. As they began this task they did not have clue what this would mean, yet they were excited about the new task.

Show... LLJ Video Segment 11—D2—*The Visual Bible*—Matthew 17:15–18 (2:09)

Rationale: In this segment the disciples have been unable to cast a demon out of the boy and now the father has brought him to Jesus to heal. The segment shows the disciples as possibly embarrassed by their inability to heal the boy.

Show... LLJ Video Segment 16—S3—The Visual Bible—Matthew 14:22-33 (3:32)

Note: The D3 clip on your DVD (Video Segment 12) is incomplete, but the S3 clip (Video Segment 16) shows the whole scene.

Rationale: In this segment Peter shows his tremendous faith as he walks on the water (high competence), yet he falls into the water when he takes his eyes off of Jesus (variable commitment).

Show... LLJ Video Segment 13—D4—*The Visual Bible*—Acts 2:36–47 (1:20)

Rationale: In this segment Peter is empowered by the Holy Spirit as he confidently and clearly shares the message of the Gospel. Note how the actor portraying Peter has changed in this segment.

Show... LLJ Video Segment 14—S1—*The Visual Bible*—Matthew 10:5–10 (:43)

Rationale: In this segment Jesus gives the disciples very clear direction as they go.

Show... LLJ Video Segment 15—S2—*The Visual Bible*—Matthew 17:18–20 (1:03)

Rationale: In this segment first notice how Jesus responds to the disciples when they ask why they could not cast out the

44

demon. The Lord is clear and direct—"You did not have enough faith." Yet also notice that *the Visual Bible* interprets this encounter as Jesus being very supportive—He reaches out and touches one of the disciples. It is the opinion of the authors that this response is consistent with the perfect character of Jesus. He was sinless, therefore, He always responded to the disciples in love, even when they made mistakes. In other words, He never lost his temper.

Show... LLJ Video Segment 16—S3—*The Visual Bible*—Matthew 14:22–33 (3:32)

Rationale: In this segment Jesus saves Peter after he falls into the water. Again, it is the opinion of the authors that Jesus' response, as shown, is consistent with His perfect character. When Peter sinks into the water, Jesus saves him and supports him as they walk together back to the boat.

Show... LLJ Video Segment 17—S4—*The Visual Bible*—Matthew 28:18–20 (1:44)

Rationale: In this segment Jesus is sending out His followers to be fishers of men. He promises that He will always be with them as they go. With the things they have learned and through the presence of the Holy Spirit in their lives, they will be ready to change the world!

EXPect Transformation

Begin by asking participants the following questions. Ask that responses be short and to the point. Pursue one or two that have the greatest likelihood of stimulating thought and learning. Remember that there are no right or wrong answers!

Ask the Group . . .

- What suggestions do you have for making the remaining weeks more meaningful, stimulating, and positive?
- What do you hope to get out of this particular session? (Share the session goals from page 43.)

EXPose Concerns

Uncover objections that group members might have regarding the concepts they have been studying. The following questions will help surface and overcome those objections. Pursue those that have the greatest relevance to your group.

Ask the Group . . .

1. What are the risks, if any, in failing to recognize and consider the developmental level of people you lead?

2. How might so-called "peak performers" become ineffective? What risks, if any, exist in labeling someone a "peak performer"?

3. What potential barriers, if any, do you recognize in your becoming a Lead Like Jesus situational leader?

4. How will those you lead ultimately assess your effectiveness as a Lead Like Jesus leader? How will you be assessed by other leaders? By God?

EXPlore Content

Encourage group members to explore honestly and openly the wealth and scope of content presented to them during their Week Five individual study. Also, encourage them to use their workbooks to maximize their exploration.

Ask the Group...

1. How is developing leaders related to leading like Jesus?

2. As a part of His vision, Jesus called His disciples to become fishers of men. What prerogatives, if any, do you as a leader have to "call" people to help you realize your own vision? How does it help if you both have a common vision?

3. Why is the Situational Leadership II® model valuable? What cautions, if any, should be exercised in using such a model?

4. How can effectiveness be measure effectively and objectively?

5. What challenges might you as a leader face in pursuing the Situational Leadership II model? How can you meet these challenges?

EXPlain Concepts

Help group members take truth into their hearts and minds by having them explain the concepts that they have been studying. Remember, the more accurate and comfortable they are in explaining these concepts succinctly in their own words, the more they have understood the truth and the more likely they are to apply it to their lives.

Ask the Group...

1. Why do you think Situational Leadership as a theory has managed to last so long?

2. Based on your study of this week's materials, how does a leader strike a balance between meeting the needs of people and achieving results?

3. From your study, what is the danger of disillusionment in those you lead?

4. What examples were used in this week's study to show how Jesus used the four leadership styles? What opportunities did you have this past week to use the four leadership styles?

EXPerience Conformation

Ask participants to engage in the following activity during the coming week and report back in the next meeting on their experiences:

1. In the coming week, keep a log of instances when you used each of the leadership styles. Note the person and his/her developmental level, what you did, how the person responded, what the outcome was, and what you learned. Then, based on your experiences and the things you learned,

state in about thirty words either your endorsement of or objections to using Situational Leadership. Consider reviewing each experience you recorded with the respective persons. Be prepared to share your experiences and what you learned with your group in the next session.

Planning For the Future — After the Session

Pray specifically for each member before the next group session.

Call all members and encourage them in their individual study of the Week Six material.

Answer any program questions that came up at today's meeting, and if appropriate contact the individual who asked it or wait until the next group meeting.

Use the following questions to evaluate your leadership:

- *Was I prepared?*
- *Was my presentation clear?*
- *Did I follow the Leader's Guide?*
- *Did I provide positive leadership?*
- *Was I a servant leader?*
- *Did I create a positive group environment?*
- *Did I help members communicate with each other?*
- *Do the members understand the purpose of the study?*

Read "Personal Preparation before the Session" on page 7 for the next group session to evaluate how much preparation you will need.

Carefully study Week Six and complete all the exercises in your own Study Guide in order to experience it fully with other group members during the next meeting.

LEAD LIKE JESUS: THE HABITS

(Session Seven – Study Guide Week Six)

SESSION GOALS

Participants will support each other by learning to . . .

- *Identify the Habits of a Lead Like Jesus leader.*
- *Recognize the Habits of solitude, prayer, and study of Scripture in the life of Jesus.*
- *Commit to enhancing the Habits in their own personal life.*

CENTRAL TRUTH

Staying true to good intentions will require continual surrender to an intimate relationship with God.

PRE—SESSION

Select and play appropriate music. Provide Personal Concerns List.

SESSION

Introduction (15 Minutes)

1. Begin session with prayer and welcome participants.

2. Have group members discuss their reflections on the Change Activity last week in light of the sections titled *Changing the Way You Act* and *Changing the People You Lead* on Day Five of this week's study.

3. Pair the group to recite their memory verse to each other.

EXPand Truth Application

Ask group members to divide into groups of three and review these two questions from the Accountability session agenda.

Ask the Group . . .

1. *Have you maintained a daily habit of prayer and time in God's Word?*

2. *Have you been anywhere this week that could be seen as a compromise?*

EXPect Transformation

Begin by asking participants the questions listed below. Ask that responses be short and to the point. Pursue one or two that have the greatest likelihood of stimulating thought and learning. Remember that there are no right or wrong answers!

Ask the Group . . .

- *What expectations did you have about this study that have not yet been met?*

- What content of this study has been easy or difficult for you?
- What was the most meaningful verse or sentence in the study this week?

EXPose Concerns

Uncover objections that group members might have about the concepts they have been studying. The following questions will help surface and overcome those objections. Pursue those that have the greatest relevance to your group.

Ask the Group... On a scale of 1–5, with 5 being the highest, rate the Habits as most/least important in your life by writing them in their priority order for you:

- Solitude
- Prayer
- Study and application of the Scripture
- Accepting and responding to God's unconditional love
- Involvement in support/accountability relationships

EXPlore Content

Show... LLJ Video Segment 18—The Habits—Solitude (Phil Hodges, 8:00)

Encourage group members to explore honestly and openly the wealth and scope of content presented to them during their individual study of the Week Six material.

Also encourage them to use their workbooks to maximize their exploration.

Ask the Group...

- What things in a leader's life make recalibration necessary?
- What are the benefits of solitude?
- How did Jesus use solitude in His life?
- What challenges do you face in making solitude a Habit in your own life?

Show... LLJ Video Segment 19—The Habits—Unconditional Love (Phil Hodges, 3:15)

Ask the Group...

- Why is accepting the unconditional love of God important in the life of a leader?
- Should a leader unconditionally love the people he or she is leading? Why?

Show... LLJ Video Segment 20—The Habits—Accountability Relationships (Ken Blanchard, 11:00)

Ask the Group...

- Why would a leader need support and accountability relationships in his or her life?

EXPlain Concepts

Help group members take truth into their hearts and minds by having them explain concepts that they have been studying. Remember that the more accurate and comfortable they are in explaining these concepts succinctly in their own words, the more they have understood the truth and the more likely they are to apply it to their lives.

Unconditional Love Activity

Depending on the size of your group you will want to choose just one of the following two activities.

Version One (3-7 group members)

Have each group member write on a sheet of paper a **brief phrase** that they wished they had heard more of when they were a child. Do not include names.

Ask the Group . . .

- Please share what you have written, but only if you feel comfortable doing so.
- Why do we like to hear these and other supportive words?
- Why would we include an activity like this in a study on leadership and the unconditional love of God?

Version Two (8 or more group members)

1. Divide the group equally. (As the leader, if there is an odd number in your group you will need to participate to make an even number.)

2. Have one half of the group place their chairs in a circle, facing inward, and be seated. The other half of the group will need to stand behind those who are seated.

3. After everyone is in place ask everyone to close their eyes and think of something they wish they had heard more of when they were a child. (Example: "You did a good job.")

4. The individuals who are sitting need to keep their eyes closed.

5. Each individual standing will place their hands on the shoulders of the person sitting in front of them. Then they will whisper quietly into that person's ear what they themselves wished they had heard more of during childhood.

6. Those standing will then move clockwise around the circle until they have spoken to everyone who is seated.

7. After everyone has gone around the circle, have the two groups change places and repeat the activity. (In smaller groups you may want to have everyone go around the circle twice to share their phrase.)

8. For the debrief, have the entire group return their chairs to their normal positions and discuss their reactions to this activity.

Ask the Group...

- Why would we include an activity like this in a study on leadership and the unconditional love of God?

EXPress Confirmation

Have the group divide into pairs to answer the following questions with their partners.

Ask the Group...

Which of the five disciplines are you practicing?

1. Solitude
2. Prayer
3. Study of Scripture
4. Faith in Unconditional Love
5. Accountability

Which disciplines will you commit to begin practicing?

EXPerience Conformation

Ask participants to engage in the following activity during the coming week and report in the next meeting on their experiences:

Who are the truth–tellers you rely upon to tell you when you are wandering off track as a Servant Leader? Take some time next week to write down their names and answer the following questions:

- How easy do you make it for your truth-tellers to share their perspectives on your behavior with you?

- Do you reward honest feedback or does it require an act of bravery to tell you a truth you might not want to hear?

Planning For the Future — After the Session

Pray specifically for each member before the next group session.

Call all members and encourage them in their individual study of the Week Seven material.

Answer for any program questions that came up at today's meeting, and if appropriate contact the individual who asked it or wait until the next group meeting.

Use the following questions to evaluate your leadership:

- Was I prepared?
- Was my presentation clear?
- Did I follow the Leader's Guide?
- Did I provide positive leadership?
- Was I a servant leader?
- Did I create a positive group environment?
- Did I help members communicate with each other?
- Do the members understand the purpose of the study?

Read "Personal Preparation before the Session" on page 7 for the next group session to evaluate how much preparation you will need.

Carefully study Week Seven and complete all the exercises in your individual Study Guide in order to full experience with other group members during the next meeting.

DISCUSS WB

Lead Like Jesus: Living as a Lead Like Jesus Leader

(Session Eight – Study Guide Week Seven)

Session Goals

Participants will support each other by learning to . . .

- Reflect on the Habits.
- Internalize Situational Leadership II® Concepts.
- Identify and write SMART goals.
- Ask for help.

Central Truth

Partnering with others is crucial for the leader who wants to *Lead Like Jesus*

Pre-Session

Select and play appropriate music. Provide Personal Concerns List.

Session

Introduction (15 Minutes)

1. Begin session with prayer and welcome participants.

2. Read the EGO's Anonymous 12–Step Process in unison.

3. Ask for volunteers to share one experience from the previous week's **EXPerience Conformation** assignment. Pursue any experiences that have unusual teaching/learning potential.

4. Pair the group to recite their memory verse to each other.

EXPand Truth Application

Allow group members time to reflect on the Habits and *Situational Leadership II* and to share, with two other group members, how the Habits are important to making one a servant leader who can practice SLII.

EXPect Transformation

Begin by asking participants the questions listed below. Ask that responses be short and to the point. Pursue one or two that have the greatest likelihood of stimulating thought and learning. Remember that there are no right or wrong answers!

Ask the Group . . .

- What one suggestion would you make to improve the group sessions for future participants?
- What one concept for the past six weeks has been the most meaningful to you?

- What one concept will be the most difficult for you to implement?
- What is the most meaningful sentence or verse in this week's study?

EXPose Concerns

Uncover objections that group members might have about the concepts they have been studying. The following questions will help surface and overcome those objections. Pursue those that have the greatest relevance to your group.

Ask the Group . . .

- How do the three skills of situational leadership (diagnosis, flexibility, and partnering for performance) help you as a leader?
- How clearly does the acronym SMART identify this strategy for goal setting? Is it easy to use/remember?
- What is the benefit of Partnering for Performance?
- What are the results of not partnering with those people you lead?

EXPlore Content

Encourage group members to explore honestly and openly the wealth and scope of content presented to them during their individual study of the Week Seven material. Also encourage them to use their workbooks to maximize their exploration.

Ask the Group . . .

- What are the benefits of stopping and starting your day with God?
- What strategies have you developed for entering your day slowly?
- How do you keep your task-oriented self from taking over?
- How do you see the role of "building people" in your current situation? What could you do differently? What needs to be strengthened?
- Explain the Situational Leadership II® Model. Which components make the most sense to you and how do you see yourself using it?
- What aspect of goal setting do you most enjoy? What seems to be the most difficult? How does the SMART Goals model fit into your everyday life?
- Based on the "How May I Help You?" meeting you had this week, what are some of the benefits of partnering with the people you lead?

EXPlain Concepts

Help group members take truth into their hearts and minds by having them explain the concepts they have been studying. Remember that the more accurate and comfortable they are in explaining these concepts succinctly in their own words, the more they have understood the truth and the more likely they are to apply it to their lives.

Instruct the group to divide into pairs and role play a "How May I Help You?" meeting. Each member will need to choose a task or goal that can be used for the role play. (Examples, learning to use a computer, becoming team leader of a new team, and the like.) Have each member of the pair follow the three steps of Partnering for Performance:

1. Teach the Situational Leadership II model.

2. Agree on key goals and objectives.

3. Diagnose Development Level for each goal.

4. Learn to match Development Level to the appropriate leadership style.

5. Deliver on what you promise.

Have members determine what the leader (in the role play activity) would need to do in order to assist the person they are leading to accomplish their desired outcomes. You may want to instruct group members to refer to Day 2-4 of week Seven for help with the role play activity.

EXPress Confirmation

Help participants incorporate what they have been learning into attitudes consistent with a *Lead Like Jesus* leader.

Ask the Group . . .

- *What did you learn about yourself through the Partnering for Performance exercise?*

- *How satisfied are you with your level of commitment to deepening the role of the Habits in your life? What can you change to improve your level of commitment?*

EXPerience Conformation

Ask participants to engage in the following activity during the coming week and report back in the next meeting on their experiences:

- *Have group members contact the teammate they partnered with this past week and set up another "How May I Help You?" meeting for continued follow up.*

PLANNING FOR THE FUTURE — AFTER THE SESSION

Pray specifically for each member before the next group session.

Call all members and encourage them in their individual study of the Week Eight material.

Answer any program questions that came up at today's meeting, and if appropriate contact the individual who asked it or wait until the next group meeting.

Use the following questions to evaluate your leadership:

- Was I prepared?
- Was my presentation clear?
- Did I follow the Leader's Guide?
- Did I provide positive leadership?
- Was I a servant leader?
- Did I create a positive group environment?
- Did I help members communicate with each other?
- Do the members understand the purpose of the study?

Read "Personal Preparation before the Session" for the next group session to evaluate how much preparation you will need.

Carefully study Week Eight and complete all the exercises in your individual Study Guide in order to experience it fully with other group members during the next meeting.

Note to Group Leader... In preparation for the "shoe mitt" activity in next week's group meeting, you will need to obtain shoe shine cloths—one for each group member. If you choose, you may purchase shoe mitts from the Center for Faithwalk Leadership at www.leadlikejesus.com.

DISCUSS WB

LEAD LIKE JESUS: MY NEXT STEPS FOR LEADING LIKE JESUS

(Session Nine – Study Guide Week Eight)

SESSION GOALS

Group members will support each other by learning to . . .

- *Practice the One-Minute apology.*
- *Prepare a personal presentation on the concepts in Lead Like Jesus.*
- *Commit to the four challenges for leaving a Lead Like Jesus legacy.*

CENTRAL TRUTH

Partnering with others is crucial for the leader who wants to *Lead Like Jesus*.

PRE—SESSION

Select and play appropriate music. Provide Personal Concerns List.

SESSION

Introduction (15 Minutes)

1. Begin session with prayer and welcome group members.

2. Read the EGO's Anonymous 12–Step Process in unison.

3. Ask for volunteers to share one experience from the previous week's **EXPerience Conformation** assignment. Pursue any experiences that have unusual teaching/learning potential.

4. Pair the group to recite their memory verse to each other.

EXPand Truth Application

Allow a brief time for group members to share what has impacted their lives the most during their Small Group Study. Ask each person to share with one or two other people in the group one or two things they have discovered about their own challenges in leading like Jesus and what they will do to meet these challenges. Allow time for a few people to share with the whole group.

EXPect Transformation

Begin by asking group members the questions listed below. Ask that responses be short and to the point. Pursue one or two that have the greatest likelihood of stimulating thought and learning. Remember that there are no right or wrong answers!

Ask the Group . . .

- To what degree has this small group experience met your expectations?
- In what ways, if any, have your expectations changed over the course of the past seven weeks?
- What do you hope to get out of this final session?
- Ask volunteers to quote one memory verse we have learned until all eight have been quoted. (As the leader you should be able to quote any verses that they are not able to quote.)

EXPose Concerns

Uncover objections that group members might have regarding the concepts they have been studying. The following questions will help surface and overcome those objections. Pursue those that have the greatest relevance to your group.

Ask the Group . . .

- Are there instances or situations where apologizing might not be advisable or appropriate?
- Should one have any concerns about seeking to leave a positive legacy? If so, what are those concerns?
- What concerns do you have as your small group study ends? What plans do you have to continue the impact of this study?

EXPlore Content

Show . . . LLJ Video Segment 21—The One Minute Apology (Ken Blanchard, 8:25)

Encourage group members to explore honestly and openly the wealth and scope of content presented to them during their individual study of the Week Eight material. Also encourage them to use their workbooks to maximize their exploration.

Ask the Group . . .

- What insights did you glean from the story of President Lincoln and Colonel Scott?
- According to the One Minute Apology, what are the components of a "real" apology?

EXPlain Concepts

Help group members take truth into their hearts and minds by having them explain the concepts they have been studying. Remember that the more accurate and comfortable they are in explaining these concepts succinctly in their own words, the more they have understood the truth and the more likely they are to apply it to their lives.

Ask the Group . . .

- Why is apologizing "a must" for a leader who wants to lead like Jesus?
- Why is it important to apologize quickly?
- What hinders one from apologizing? How can these hindrances be overcome?

EXPress Confirmation

Help group members incorporate what they have been learning into attitudes consistent with a *Lead Like Jesus* leader.

Have group members review the "My Lead Like Jesus Presentation" they completed on Day Two of Week Eight. Use this as the basis for preparing a two–minute overview of the concepts of Lead Like Jesus that could be shared readily and with confidence and precision. Instruct members to get into pairs and share their presentation.

Ask the Group . . .

- *What did you learn about yourself and Christ's expectations of you from the Readiness Exam? What areas will require special attention, if any?*

- *What did you learn about yourself as you studied the Four Challenges of Leaving a Lead Like Jesus Legacy? What decisions, if any, did you make in light of this understanding?*

- *What commitments did you make in Day 5?*

- *What will you do to make the lessons you have learned in this study a part of your daily life as a leader?*

Show . . . LLJ Video Segment 22—Closing Words (Ken Blanchard)

EXPerience Conformation

Encourage group members to participate in one or more of the following activities:

1. Make a list of persons to whom you need to apologize for something. Indicate beside each person's name that for which you need to apologize. In a third column, identify the best way to follow through with the apology, and in a fourth column, write a one-sentence prayer expressing your willingness to make an unqualified, unconditional apology quickly.

2. Shoe Shine Activity:

- Have shoe cloths or mitts on hand.

- Have everyone stand in a circle.

- Read John 13:3-5, 12-17. [BIBLE]

- Say: "If we are going to Lead Like Jesus, it is vital that we practice what Jesus taught. We are going to demonstrate our desire to be servant leaders by shining the shoes of our fellow group members." (Pass out cloths or mitts.)

- As the leader, you will want to demonstrate how to get down on your knees and shine the shoes of someone in the group. When you have finished give the person a hug.

- Encourage everyone to participate.

- Pray that all group members will begin to practice the principles that they have learned as they begin to Lead Like Jesus *in their family, at work and in their community.*

Planning for the Future — After the Session

Pray for each group member as your formal study of these truths comes to a close.

Call all members and encourage them in their quest to *Lead Like Jesus*.

Consider forming another *Lead Like Jesus* group or an accountability group with others from the current class.

Encourage your apprentice from this class to seek people to participate in a *Lead Like Jesus* group that he or she will lead.

Encourage your apprentice to participate in an accountability group.

Answer any program questions that came up at today's meeting, and if appropriate contact the individual who asked it.

Evaluate your role as a facilitator for this group, and consider those areas where you might need to grow.

Lead Like Jesus!

For More Information

The Center for Faithwalk Leadership is a non-profit organization that challenges and equips people to *Lead Like Jesus*.

For more information on the Center for Faithwalk Leadership and its *Lead Like Jesus* seminars and resources, contact:

www.leadlikejesus.com

1229 Augusta West Parkway
Augusta, Georgia 30909
voice (706) 863-8494
toll free (800) 383-6890
fax (706) 863-9372

Additional Resources for the Group Leader and Group Members

Lead Like Jesus: Beginning the Journey Resources

The Servant Leader, by Ken Blanchard and Phil Hodges

Leadership By The Book, by Ken Blanchard, Bill Hybles and Phil Hodges

We Are The Beloved, by Ken Blanchard

***Lead Like Jesus* Shoe Shine Mitts** for the shoe shine activity in Week 8, can be purchased by contacting the Center For Faithwalk Leadership at www.leadlikejesus.com.

***Lead Like Jesus* Partnering for Performance Worksheets:** These worksheets are designed to assist the individual who would like to have a practical tool for implementing the concepts of Partnering for Performance (See Week 5) as a Lead Like Jesus leader. More information on the use of this tool and ordering information visit the Center For Faithwalk Leadership website at www.leadlikejesus.com.

Training Resources

Additional ***Lead Like Jesus:* Beginning the Journey Study Guides** can be purchased through the Center For Faithwalk Leadership, www.leadlikejesus.com or through your local Christian bookstore.

***Lead Like Jesus:* Beginning the Journey** video segments on VHS may purchased by contacting the Center For Faithwalk Leadership.

***Lead Like Jesus:* A Leadership Encounter Workshop** is an opportunity for participants to experience much of the same content and material as found in the Lead Like Jesus: Beginning the Journey Group Study, only in a two–day or three–day format. This workshop is ideal for a church staff, work team, or any group of leaders who would like to learn more about how to Lead Like Jesus. The event is led by a member of the Center For Faithwalk Leadership Team or a facilitator certified by the Center For Faithwalk Leadership. Many organizations have found it is beneficial to send their key leaders through this event, prior to the roll-out of the Lead Like Jesus: Beginning the Journey eight week study. This workshop has been conducted over the past several years across the country resulting in the lives of leaders being changed. If you would like more information about this workshop and other training opportunities offered by the Center For Faithwalk Leadership, please contact us at 800-383-6890 or on the web at www.leadlikejesus.com.

Situational Leadership II®
Additional Resources

As discussed in both the *Lead Like Jesus: Beginning the Journey* Group Study guide and the Leader's Guide, Situational Leadership II® was developed by Ken Blanchard and Paul Hersey as a model for leadership behavior. There has been extensive research and development done over the years which will add the group leader in understanding, teaching and application of these principles. Listed below are a few of those resources:

Leadership And the One Minute Manager, Ken Blanchard, Patricia Zigarmi and Drea Zigarmi, 1985

Management of Organizational Behavior, Ken Blanchard, Paul Hersey